Feed My Sheep

By

HAROLD R. GIELOW

All quotations of Bible texts are taken from the King James version except as noted.

Copyright 2004
by H. Gielow, author, without whose written permission, no part of this book may be copied.

ISBN 1-894581-10-5

Cover Design: Don Connelly
Calligraphy by: Carol Gray

HIS SERVICE PUBLISHING / SERVICE PUBLICATIONS
Florida 33326   / Ottawa, Canada

Dedication

This book was written shortly after the death of my eldest son. I am not certain what prompted me to write such a work at such a time. Perhaps it was that I was more introspective than is my norm, especially about those things in life which are truly important. Though I did not consciously dwell on the death of my son in an emotionally destructive way, it is clear that the loss of that relationship had a profound impact on me, even though I had become well acquainted with broken relationships due to death through my years in the military.

This is, in essence, the focus of this book - man's relationships to others and to God, the impact of a broken relationship, and the incredibly fulfilling experience of finding spiritual and emotional health through getting those relationships right.

This book is dedicated to the memory of my son, Harold Richard Gielow Junior, with grateful thanks to my wife Elizabeth Baker Gielow, my father and mother, and to my brother and sisters, cousins and friends who all, through their example of love and friendship, encouraged and inspired its writing.

A special thanks is due to Eithne Nunez and my mother, Laura Frances Gielow. whose selfless devotion to the message and their untiring efforts and dedication in spreading God's message of love, ensured its completion.

Harold R. Gielow

Prologue

Simon sat adrift in thought and remorse so intense that all else was drowned in its depths. Even the nearby chatter of Thomas, Nathaniel and the others was dull and remote, as if coming from the distant shore mixed with the sounds of the wind and waves. Each wave that lifted the old weather beaten boat towards the heavens brought a flood of joyous memories, only to recede as the boat sank ignominiously back towards earth and Simon, with it, back into the trough of despair. "How could I have denied Him after all that I witnessed?" Simon thought, as a groan involuntarily escaped his lips. "Did I not tell Him that I was a sinful man? Why did He trust me? Why didn't He just leave me where He found me instead of showing me the wonders of the possible through trusting him only, to leave me alone?"

The similarity of the present situation with Simon's first meeting with Jesus brought into sharp focus that first miraculous encounter. Now, like then, he had fished all night, using all the skills and knowledge acquired through years of fishing the sea, with not one catch to show for the calluses on his hands or his aching back. Jesus had been preaching to the crowd on the shore while Simon was washing the nets after the fruitless night of fishing. He had stepped into Simon's boat and asked to be taken out a little way from the shore, for the crowd was pressing Him. "Put out into the deep water and let down your nets for a catch." Simon remembered His words as if it were yesterday. His blistered hands and tired muscles from last night's fishing reminded him, as well, of his response on that first morning with the Lord, but he had done as Jesus said. Simon recalled his joy and amazement with the miracle that followed, and then, as the boat slid into another trough, recalled a feeling more in tune with his present state. "Depart from me, for I am a sinful man, Oh Lord." "His eyes pierced into my very soul," Simon recalled.

Simon's mind raced forward as the boat creaked and moaned and began to rise on the next wave. "What glory we beheld as He was transfigured before us," Simon thought, his heart nearly bursting with the remembered joy of that sacred moment, and then nearly rending in two as He also recalled seeing himself in the light of the holiness of God. The boat slid into another trough as Simon played back the scene, for the thousandth time, of his denial of the Lord. A gentle breeze began to blow, drying the tears on Simon's face, as he lifted his eyes and looked towards the shore. Someone was standing there, their form barely visible as the dawn was just now breaking, the sun rising on the shore's Eastern horizon and casting its glow on the now shimmering waters. The man called out to them, His voice drifting across the waves in the stillness of the morning, "Children, you do not have any fish do you?" "No!" Thomas blurted out, kicking the empty net as if to emphasize his point. Simon, still lost in his grief, barely noticed the exchange. "Cast the net on the right hand side of the boat and you will find a catch." Simon looked at John, his heart beginning to race, and saw in John's eyes the same question that his own heart was screaming. "Could it be?" Hurriedly, he picked up the net with the others and cast it upon the waters, leaning this way and that as it sank, peering intently and hoping expectantly. It seemed like forever as Simon waited for the net to sink, as if eternity hung in the balance and this cast was his last hope. "Pull it in! Pull it in!" Simon cried, and as they grabbed the ropes and pulled, they went taut with the familiar feel of a great number of fish. "It *is* the Lord," cried John, and Simon, no sooner had these words left John's mouth, was in the water furiously swimming towards the Lord.

    The others followed, dragging the net full of fish behind them and, when they arrived at the shore, found a charcoal fire prepared with fish placed upon it and bread. Simon looked at the fire and then on his Lord. It was around just such a fire that he had denied Him. Jesus said, "Bring me some of the fish which you have now caught." Simon went over to the net and drew it in to the shore. Afterwards, Jesus broke bread with them. Simon recalled his boastful statement at that last supper before his denial and his Lord's crucifixion; "Even though all may fall away, yet I will not." As he was recalling his boast, as if reading his thoughts, Jesus spoke to him. "Simon, son of John, do you love me with a Godly love more than these?" Simon's heart was pierced recalling his boast, his denial, and his failed attempt to follow the Lord in his own strength as Simon, son of flesh and blood, not Peter, the rock, born of the Spirit. "Yes Lord, You know that I love you (with a warm, longing love." Simon looked down at the ground. He had not yet looked into the eyes of the Lord. "Perhaps He will think that I misunderstood Him," Simon reasoned. Jesus said to him, "Feed my lambs." Looking on him intently, Jesus then asked him, "Simon, son of John, do you love me (with a Godly love)?"

Again Simon's heart was pierced because He asked him, not if he loved him more than the others loved Him, but only did he love Him. More humbly, Simon replied, "Yes Lord, You know that I love you (with a warm longing love)." Jesus said, "Shepherd my sheep." Then Simon looked into the eyes of his Savior and heard Him speak yet again. "Simon, son of John, *do* you love me (with a warm, longing love?" With this, Simon's heart became completely broken, and he cried out, as in a cry for help, "Lord, You know all things. You know that I love you (with a warm, longing love)." Jesus said, "Feed my little sheep."

The Search for Significance

Man spends his entire life in search of significance. He seeks affirmation from family, friends, and even from his own conscience. He seeks it through achievement at work, by the acquisition of wealth, and in countless other avenues.

In spite of the Christian's assurance of God's proven love for His creatures in that, '...while we were yet sinners, Christ died for us,' man still seeks assurance of acceptance, love and value. Each of us, if we have accepted Christ's sacrifice for us, is endowed by our creator with a limitless potential for good, for we are filled with the very spirit of the living God. Yet this potential will never be realized until it is offered in the spirit of God, fully to His service, and in a spirit of self-sacrificial love. We will never truly find our significance until we lose ourselves in God's love.

Man's search for significance and purpose has led him, both individually and collectively, into a wide variety of pursuits. No one book of the Bible more expressively details our various endeavors in this area than Ecclesiastes, a book concerned with the purpose and value of human life. After exploring the pursuits of man in pleasure, great works, riches, wisdom, and mirth, the author concludes that they are all mere 'vanity and vexation of spirit'. King Solomon is believed to have been the author of Ecclesiastes, of whom the Bible says, "There was none like thee before thee, neither after thee shall any arise like unto thee." He was the recipient of the divine gifts of wisdom and understanding (I Kings 3:12). Yet many, before and after Solomon, have sought to answer the same question. What is that good which man should accomplish under the sun?

For Epictetus, a great philosopher and teacher at Rome, the answer was to be secure, happy, and to do what one pleases without restraint and without compulsion. For Aristotle, the renowned teacher of wisdom in ancient Greece, the rational pursuit of self-interest, one's own happiness, was the greatest good, happiness being a whole life well lived, attaining all those goods which one really needs.

Our own Founding Fathers, drawing heavily on both Greek philosophy and the Roman law tradition with its emphasis on a body of free and independent individuals within a unitary state, developed a religiously grounded faith in the individual's right of self determination of ethical action. We see this codified in the Declaration of Independence as the 'unalienable right' to the pursuit of happiness. The purpose of government was to secure the 'natural rights' of the individual to life, liberty, and the pursuit of happiness.

It is one thing to declare that each individual has an unalienable right to happiness, but it is quite another to declare how one can achieve this state. With no more guide than the declaration that happiness is our birthright, natural man looks to the physical world for its fulfillment. His yearning for happiness is transformed by his rational pursuit to fill the void created by its absence, and, if this pursuit is not restrained, it leads to his unlimited quest for self worth through achievement, recognition, and security by means that afford him power or influence over others - through wealth, force, and knowledge.

These egoistic (self-gratifying) ends are modified, constrained, and transformed into more limited ends by our interactions and activities as part of a family, community, state, and ultimately global community. The transformation wrought by these influences alone, however, cannot lead to a basic change in the end sought - the pleasing of self.

The Bits and Bridles of Desire

A world of competing desires fueled by self interest over which no universally recognized, legitimate authority exists with the ability to enforce a normative standard is a chaotic world where might makes right. The constraining influence of social structures was the Hobbesian justification for a powerful state as a check on the passions of man which, if left unbridled, would lead to a perpetual state of chaos and war.

John Locke and other political philosophers of the Enlightenment era argued that such a powerful state was unnecessary as men would realize their "natural identity of interests," or that one could best achieve one's desires in a social context by allowing for the desires of others to be met as well.

Competition for scarce resources, a problem articulated by Thomas Malthus in 1798 in his work *Population* constrains man's ability to meet his desires. The limiting feature, however, is not so much scarcity of resources as it is the boundless nature of our appetites or desires for self pleasure.

According to the United Nations, the world population increased from 1 billion in 1800 to 5.9 billion in 1997. It is expected to reach over 11 billion by 2100. Ninety-five percent of this future growth will take place in the poorest countries, many of which cannot even feed their present populations. But the real issue here, according to the UN, is not overpopulation, but rather over consumption. The developed countries, with over 20% of the earth's population, now consume 60% of its resources.

An article in the February 1994 issue of the Atlantic Monthly titled "The Coming Anarchy" predicted the following scenario: "Nations break up under a tidal flow of refugees from environmental and social disaster. As borders crumble, another type of boundary is erected - a wall of disease. Wars are fought over scarce resources, especially water, and war itself becomes continuous with crime."

Edmund Burke, the English political philosopher, addressed the societal implications of man's unchecked appetites best in the following statement. "In every society, a controlling influence on will and appetite must be placed somewhere, and the less of it there is within, the more there must be without. It is ordained in the eternal constitution of things that men of intemperate minds cannot be free. Their passions forge their fetters."

Man can never satisfy his diverse, innate needs apart from his creator. He craves, in his deepest being, to be worthy, accepted, and loved, but no human relationship can possibly give him total, unconditional, selfless love and acceptance. This love is experienced only through a close fellowship with God, without which he can never experience this love, for "God is Love." It is His love which compels us to obedience, not of necessity through force, but rather through its overwhelming evidence as He reveals Himself to us.

God's Plan

A free and democratic society is incompatible with a secularized, utilitarian philosophy without some strong, external, controlling influence. This external influence can take many forms. Family, tradition, religion, law, and government are examples. None of these, however, are ultimately sufficient because none of them fully address or satisfy our inner longings and needs.

When the ends of utilitarian philosophy become divorced from a belief in a spiritual, eternal reality, and the ultimate end becomes temporal happiness, the very meaning of what is really good for us changes. Aristotle viewed happiness as a whole life well lived, rationally choosing those things which are really good for us. The very concept of what is really good for us, those things which we need by virtue of our human nature, obviously changes when we discount the spiritual, eternal nature of man.

External constraints may serve as a societal glue for some time but are, in the end, insufficient without an understanding of man's innate capacity to experience God and to know Him, and to thereby know his own spiritual nature. Without this knowledge, man can never truly feel fulfilled for he cannot meet his innate spiritual need to know God and, through that knowledge, understand his own eternal worth, value, and purpose in God's plan for his being. Religion is also insufficient, as it is quite possible to display all the forms of religion and still exercise no faith or trust in, nor know God (deny the power thereof).

It is only by His unmerited favor (grace) that we can be justified. It is only by claiming this grace, through faith, that we can feel secure, know that we are truly secure, and act on that knowledge to reflect God's glorious character of love to others. It is only through faith that we can attain the hope of our highest good - love. Through the divine message of salvation we may believe, by believing we may hope, and by hoping we may love.

We become enabled to accept and love others unconditionally only when we ourselves have experienced this unconditional acceptance and are empowered by the indwelling presence of God to share this with others.

Secular, humanistic philosophy and utilitarianism, placing its faith in man's capacity to know truth through reason, leaves morality, justice and behavior to the discretion of enlightened man. In his book, *"The Search For Significance,"* Robert McGee puts it thus: "Living without God's divine truth, humanity sinks lower and lower in depravity, blindly following a philosophy that intends to heighten the dignity of man, but which instead lowers him to the level of the animals."

Reason vs. Revelation

Man cannot know spiritual truth apart from God. While God, His nature, even His eternal godhead, can be known with certainty from created reality through human reason, it is only through His revelation that spiritual truth can be known.

Just as science looks to the physical world for truth, religion looks to the spiritual world for truth. Spiritual truth is not to be found in empirical data, but just as there are physical laws, so too there are spiritual laws. And just as the concepts contained in physical laws provide meaning, organization, and purpose to disparate physical events, so too, spiritual laws provide meaning, organization and purpose to spiritual events. To understand these spiritual laws, man must train himself to see with the eyes of the spirit. To do this, he must first have the indwelling presence of God's Holy Spirit. In Romans 7:7, we read, "By the law is the knowledge of sin." The rational man can know this full well, but it is only through the spirit that comes the revelation of truth and the ability to overcome our sinful nature.

The True Age of Enlightenment

John Locke's early writings have been regarded as primers of enlightenment philosophy and natural law theory upon which the Founding Fathers drew heavily as the basis for the Declaration of Independence, the Constitution, and our democratic system of government.

The writings of his later years, years which were devoted to the study of the Holy Scriptures, should be read as a summary to his years of study and thought on political philosophy. The following is a quote from his essay, *Christian Revelation, The Sure Standard of Morality.*

Whatsoever should thus be universally useful as a standard to which men should conform their manners must have its authority either from reason or revelation. Such a law of morality Jesus Christ hath given in the New Testament; but by the latter of these ways, by revelation, we have from Him a full and sufficient rule for our direction and conformable to that of reason. But the truth and obligation of its precepts have their force, and are put past doubt to us, by the evidence of His mission. He was sent by God: His miracles show it; and the authority of God in His precepts cannot be questioned. Here morality has a sure standard, that revelation vouches, and reason cannot gainsay nor question."

Solomon's search for life's purpose through the book of Ecclesiastes ends with these words of wisdom. "Let us hear the conclusion of the whole matter. Fear God and keep His commandments: for this is the whole duty of man." What could be more plainly stated than this? Moses, likewise, concluded his giving of the law:

> For the commandment which I give you today is not too difficult for you, nor is it out of your reach. It is not in heaven, that you should say, 'Who will go up to heaven for us to get it, that we may observe it?' Nor is it beyond the sea, that you should say, 'Who will cross the sea for us to get it for us and make us hear it, that we may observe it?' But the word is very near you, in your

mouth and in your heart, that you may observe it. See, I have set before you today life and prosperity, and death and adversity." (Deut 30:11-15)

One of America's best known humorists, Mark Twain, emphasized this truth when he said, "Most people are bothered by those passages of the scripture which they cannot understand. But as for me, the scriptures which trouble me most are those which I do understand."

Some things are known only to God, but through the scripture we have His clear revelation to us for all to read and store up in our hearts, and in Jesus Christ we have God the Father's greatest revelation and fulfillment of the Word.

The Commandment of Love

Let us hear then the words of Christ. "And one of the scribes came and heard them arguing, and recognizing that He had answered them well, asked Him, 'What commandment is the foremost of all?' Jesus answered,

> The foremost is, Hear, O Israel. The Lord your God is one Lord; and you shall love the Lord your God with all your heart, and with all your soul, and with all your mind, and with all your strength. The second is this, you shall love your neighbor as yourself. There is no other commandment greater than these."

It is our duty to obey God's commandments. God Himself, through His son, has revealed to us that the whole law is embodied in the one great commandment to love God with our whole being and others as ourselves. It is through obedience that we are empowered to fulfill our purpose of reflecting God's glorious character of love to the world around us, to bring good news to the afflicted, to bind up the broken hearted, to proclaim liberty to captives and freedom to prisoners - to reconcile man to God. Man's prescription for happiness is the rational pursuit of self interest. God's is the pursuit of the best interest of others with one's whole being.

The Gospel of Love

We are commanded, empowered, compelled and created to love. We are commanded to love by our Lord. We are empowered to do so by God's unconditional acceptance of us through Christ and our obedience to Him through faith. We are compelled to do so by the Spirit of God within us and the love of God for us. We were created so that, through our intellect, free will, and emotions we might reflect the glorious character of Christ and reconcile others to Him.

We are commanded to love, not just with our minds but with our whole being. It is not an option. If we are to reflect His character and be conformed to His image, we must love for, as the apostle John says, "He that loveth not knoweth not God, for God is love." (1 John 4:8) If we are to be obedient children, we must love, for this is God's greatest commandment and it is our duty to be obedient in performing it. If we are to have the blessed assurance of our faith, we must love, for "We know that we have passed out of death into life because we love the brethren." (1 John 3:14)

If we are to experience the full joy of God's forgiveness we must love, for we pray "...and forgive those who trespass against us," and true forgiveness proceeds from love. If we are to experience God, His fullness and His presence in our lives, we must love for "if we love one another, God abides in us, and His love is perfected in us." (1 John 4:12) If we are to be anything for Christ, then we must love, for without love we are nothing. (1 Corinthians 13:2)

If God is to be God, then He must demand that we love Him, for love is the eternal highest good, and He must want that good for all of His children or He would be acting contrary to His very nature. God must demand love, for love is the fulfillment of the law.

If God must command that we love, it would be the height of absurdity for us to believe that He would not also enable us to love. If we fail in love, it is not God's failure, but ours. The command, at one stroke, destroys all excuses as it contains both the unequivocal, unambiguous demand and the promise of the provision to meet the demand.

God's Love vs. Man's Love

The love commanded by God is not love as the world knows love. First, it is rooted in obedience. To love is to obey the law, and love, though it may escape definition in many ways except by describing its character, is obedience of the law.

Conversely, natural love is rooted in self-will or desire. One might argue that this is no different as all action proceeds from inner desire, but the natural man is incapable of loving as God loves for this very reason. He has only his self will and competing desires to wrestle with. For the Christian who is in-filled with the very Spirit of God, "...it is God which worketh in you both to will and to do His good pleasure." (Phil. 2:13)

It is by first being obedient in submission to the urgings of the Holy Spirit in us that we are enabled to truly love. It is only through obedience, forsaking self-will, that we can love, and it is only through the Spirit of God within us that this obedience is possible. To love as God loves requires that we take self-will and nail it to the cross so that it is no longer we who live and will, but Christ in us who lives and wills, and our only desire is to be completely submitted to Him.

Secondly, this love is not simply volitional, nor simply emotional, nor yet simply physical. It involves our whole being and all of the capabilities of each part of our being. This is impossible with man, but with God, 'all things are possible.'

To love with our whole mind must include the idea of loving with the whole capability of our mind. This, however, is impossible without the Spirit, for spiritual perception and knowledge would be lacking. We would be left with that knowledge which is acquired only through our physical perceptions, which knowledge is often flawed and incomplete as "...the natural man receiveth not the things of the Spirit of God for they are foolishness to him; neither can he know them, because they are spiritually discerned." ((1 Cor. 2:14)

Neither can we love with all of the capabilities of our physical strength without God, for it is God who "shall renew" our strength.(Is.40:31) Samson's great physical strength did not lie in his long hair. His unshaven head was simply the symbol of his obedience to God as one especially consecrated to God - a Nazerite. Nor can we love with our whole spirit without God, for without the love and unconditional acceptance of God, we can never truly love and accept ourselves as we should, much less others. Our deep, spiritual, inner need for love, acceptance, and worth cannot be met outside of God's grace.

Erotic love and brotherly love are really only self-love. They seek to possess the object of love as the one and only love because the object of love presents itself as pleasing, either sensually or emotionally. They love to meet or fulfill personal desire, whereas in God's love our desires, our wills, are shaped through obedience. To put it more plainly, with natural man, love is an expression of desire, but with spiritual man his desires are an expression of his love which is made perfect through, and is obedience to, the will of God.

Empowered to Love

We are empowered to love as we ought by obedience through faith. It has been said that love is not a feeling but is rather a commitment. Our emotional and spiritual commitments, however, are necessarily connected to our mental/rational commitments and our actions. Proverbs 16:3 says, *"Commit thy works unto the Lord and thy thoughts shall be established."* James 2:22 says, *"Seest though how faith wrought (operated) with his works and by works was faith made perfect (complete)."*

To act in faith means to rely completely on God. To act in a loving manner, whether we feel loving or not, requires a commitment to obedience to and reliance on God. When we make this mental commitment to act in obedience to God, regardless of the cost to us personally, and then follow through on this commitment, God "establishes" our thoughts by showing Himself to be always true to His word.

When we see His purpose and His will worked out in our lives and in the lives of those we love, not because of our abilities or our actions but through our total reliance on Him, our faith is made "complete." The evidence of His personal presence in our lives to work all things out for good is made clear. We more fully realize, not just through intellectual belief but through personal experience, that we can truly, totally rely on God, and this enables us to love Him and others more completely.

As we act in obedience to God, He shows us how completely He meets our deepest needs and we come to realize that it is only through Him that those needs can truly be met. We come to realize that, truly, in Him we live and move and have our being (Acts 17:28), for only through His indwelling presence are we made complete as by Him all things consist (Col 1:17). This realization is necessarily connected with the development of strong emotions as well, for we are always most passionate about those things for which we care deeply - our deep, inner needs.

Our emotional commitment grows by the exercise of our faith, and our faith comes by hearing, and this by the word of God (Rom 10:17). To grow in our commitment to God, we must exercise our faith, and to exercise our faith we need to fill our minds and hearts with the word of God. We must meditate on God's word day and night and, figuratively, bind them upon our hands and put them as frontlets between our eyes and write them upon the posts of our homes and on our gates (Deut 6:8-9). Jesus said, *"The light of the body is the eye: if therefore thine eye be single, thy whole body shall be full of light. But if thine eye be evil, thy whole body shall be full of darkness."* (Mat 6:22-23) Paul admonishes us to fill our minds with *" ...whatsoever things are true, whatsoever things are honest, whatsoever things are just, whatsoever things are pure, whatsoever things are lovely, whatsoever things are of good report..."* (Phil 4:8)

There is an old saying in computer lingo- GIGO. It stands for "garbage in, garbage out." The same principal, in many ways, applies to human beings. We will become, in some sense, what we choose to meditate and reflect on. If we constantly dwell on our failures, we will likely become very hesitant to take any risks that might lead to more or, if we do act, it may tend to be in a half hearted manner, precipitating the very failure that we fear. If we entertain sinful thoughts, we will be much more likely to act in a sinful manner. All action, unless it is instinctive, begins in our thought lives. Proverbs 23:7 tells us, *"As a man thinketh in his heart, so is he." Proverbs 4:23 further tells us to "Keep thine heart with all diligence for out of it are the issues of life."*

To become more committed to God, to love Him with our whole being, we must exercise our faith, and to exercise our faith we must fill our minds with the things of God and, through obedience, begin the walk of faith. Then will God *"...open unto you the windows of heaven and pour you out a blessing that there shall not be room enough to receive it."* (Mal 3:10) Feed your mind with the word of God. Meditate upon it. Dwell upon it. Develop a passion for God's word and the habit of putting it into practice. God has promised that His word will not return void. Let His word become part of your very being.

Compelled by the Spirit

We are compelled to love by the Spirit of God within us and by the love of God for us. Total, Godly love does indeed start with that mental commitment, but more importantly, there must first be a relationship formed by that act of obedience and commitment in accepting Christ as our Lord and Savior. At that moment, the Spirit of God indwells us and begins to reveal to us those areas of our lives which we need to commit to Him. God tells us,"...*behold, I will pour out my spirit upon you, I will make known my words to you.*" (Prov 1:23) God reveals the hidden truths of His word to us through His spirit. Jeremiah 31:33 says, "*I will put my law in their inward parts, and write it in their hearts.*"

In His word, through the agency of the Holy Spirit, God reveals to us His will for our lives. In our daily walk, God brings the revealed word to our remembrance so that we perceive not only with the eyes of the flesh but also with the vision of the spirit. He brings it to our remembrance at precisely the right moment and precisely the right place to fulfill His purpose in us and through us.

The Spirit leads us to the point of decision to obey or disobey. It does not alone compel. It is only through obedience that God, because of His infinite love for us, proves Himself to be always faithful and reveals even more of Himself to us. As the prophet Isaiah teaches us, "Whom shall He teach knowledge? And whom shall He make to understand doctrine? Them that are weened from the milk, and drawn from the breast. For precept must be upon precept, precept upon precept; line upon line, line upon line; here a little, and there a little." (Isaiah 28: 9-10)

As we commit ourselves to act in obedience, God directs our thoughts and emotions, enabling us to more fully love Him, and further reveals Himself to us. He gives us a heart to know Him (Jer 24:7). Our passion for God and His word grows as we act in obedience to the urging of the Spirit and see God work in and through our lives as we rely on Him.

This compelling, then, is not one of necessity, but one of overwhelming evidence of God's faithfulness to His word when we act in obedience to Him. It is this overwhelming evidence which cuts like a knife to circumcise our very hearts. Through the urging of the Spirit, our obedience, and God's faithfulness, we become even more dedicated to God in our very feelings.

Created By Him and For Him

We are created so that, through our intellect, free will, and emotions, we might reflect the glorious character of Christ and reconcile others to Him. With all of our talents, abilities, and assets, we are unable to meet our own needs for security, worth, purpose, and love. It is only in giving ourselves completely to God, body, mind, and soul, that we will ever truly find real life, real liberty, or real happiness. To love Him with our whole being, and through that relationship to be enabled to truly love others, is our highest good, for it is what we were made for.

The Nature and Character of Love

The nature of love is that which it truly, in its essence, is. It is that definition of love which encompasses all other definitions. The true nature of love is obedience of the law. Without love, we are nothing. Without the indwelling presence of God, we cannot love as we ought. Our motivations have their genesis in our needs and wants and our desire to meet them. Even our acts of altruism can be traced to our desire to be accepted and praised by others or to feel justified in our own minds by proof of our goodness. This, however, is also vanity. There is none good save God. We are all sinners justified only by the blood of Jesus and His sacrifice. It is His righteousness that God sees in us, not our own. Our righteousness is as *'filthy rags'*. All of our works, no matter how good they may be or how many may benefit from them, matter not to God as a means to justify us in His sight. Jesus, and only Jesus, is our sole justification. We may understand all knowledge and all mysteries, and use that talent to help others, but if we have not love, we are nothing. We may be the most eloquent speaker the world has ever heard, able to move the hearts and minds of others to do great and mighty works, but without love, it profits us nothing.

We can give all that we have, even our very lives, to the service of others, even giving our bodies to be burned, and if we have not love we are nothing. Without love, it is all nothing - of absolutely no consequence and valueless - in regards to our worth or value in God's eyes.

God help us. How can anyone stand in the presence of a holy God who calls us to be perfect even as He is perfect? Praise God, we can. Not in our own righteousness. Not in our own works, but through the sacrifice of God's son. We cannot love as we ought, but Christ in us and through us can. It is only through obedience to the urgings of the Spirit that we can love as we ought so that it is not we who will, but Christ in us who wills.

Have you quenched the Spirit? Have you denied the Spirit's urging to love the unlovely, to forgive those who mistreat you, or to be patient and loving when your carnal nature was screaming within you to return insult for insult? In our own strength, these things are impossible, but the Spirit speaks to our hearts, hearts born in selfishness, to be unselfish. It is only through obedience to the urgings of the Spirit that our motivations can be pure, for it is only in this way that our motivations can come from a source of purity - the Holy Spirit living within us.

God's Nature Revealed

It is through obedience to the urgings of the Spirit that God enables us to grow in love for, through obedience, God reveals Himself, His nature, and His will to us. That His nature is infinite power, infinite wisdom, and infinite goodness we all attest, but through obedience and the continued revelation of God to us we experience them first hand. Moreover, it is only through our obedience to His revealed will, even though that revelation may be only in part and that part which we have been prepared to receive, that we may see His nature revealed, for through our obedience He shows Himself to be faithful.

He shows us that His way is the way that truly leads to our happiness. It is through this revelation of His nature that the evidence of His superior authority is clearly displayed to our reason. If, then, happiness is our aim, it becomes irrational to presume that we could attain this state through any other means. We are morally obliged to obey, as obligation is no more than a restriction of our liberty to use any means to obtain the ends we seek, and reason clearly shows that our happiness can be obtained through no other means. This, however, does not alone compel us to obedience. It does, if only for the brief moment of the revelation, fix our eyes on Christ and compel us to decide - will I look down at the waves thrashing about my feet and be distracted from my goal, or will I continue to see my Lord and His will and direction for my life? The moment we take our eyes off of the Savior, our reasoning is impaired by self-will and misperception.

It is only through continued obedience to God's revealed will that our spiritual myopia can be corrected and, just as our short sighted vision returns the moment our eyeglasses are removed, even so our spiritual short-sightedness returns the moment we take our eyes off the Savior.

We often, like Peter, ask the Lord to reassure us in the storms of life, to help us to walk above the raging waves of life's troubles. We also often are prone, like Peter, to become distracted from our goal - to walk with Christ through the storm, constantly moving towards Him, and become overwhelmed by life's troubles.

Do you want your love for God to grow? Obey Him. Those who love Him obey His voice. Do they obey Him because they love Him? Perhaps rather they love Him because through their obedience He reveals more of Himself, His nature, His goodness, His wisdom, and His power to them in a personal way. To love God is to obey Him, for it is only through our obedience that He will reveal Himself to us and, through this revelation, allow us to love Him and, through Him, others as we should.

When there is an area of our lives in which God has clearly revealed to us a need for obedience, He is asking for us to let Him reveal more of Himself to us, even when the change seems a small thing. Small or large, obedience is always required to experience the reality of God in our lives. Proverbs 1:7 says, *"The fear of the Lord is the beginning of knowledge."* Proverbs 9:10 amplifies this by saying, *"The beginning of wisdom is the fear of the Lord, and knowledge of the Holy One is understanding."*

Awe and reverence for the Omnipotent God, and our submission to His authority, is a critical first step to or beginning of our knowledge of the awesome nature of our loving Father. Even after a lifetime of walking with Him, we still see only a glimpse of His glory. To fear God and keep His commandments is our duty. That duty, however, becomes our joy as He continues to reveal Himself to us through our obedience, and this causes us to love Him more. Perhaps, at times, we need a renewed sense of awe and respect for the Almighty God in order that we might come to more fully know Father God.

Only God can take the neediness out of our relationships because only God can satisfy our deepest needs. We are enabled to love others as we should when we experience God's unconditional love and acceptance which frees us from seeking fulfillment of these needs in our relationships with others. He frees us to love as we should by making us totally secure in Him and completely worthy through Him, for He becomes our high tower and our righteousness.

Love is Patient
(Latin- Patiri - to suffer)
(Those thoughts, emotions, and expressions which proceed from an inner motivation of desiring the best for others. The quality or habit of enduring without complaint.)

The command to love is not solely a call to action, but also one to forbearance, which often requires a much greater strength of will, or more correctly a greater degree of submission to God's will.

No greater example can be shown than that of the patience of Christ as He prayed in the garden until sweat drops of blood from His agonizing heart came forth, and then as He was beaten and scourged without uttering a word in His defense. Such forbearance could possibly be conceived of one who was powerless, but even then it is hard to believe. How much more incredible in one who could but speak the word and a host of angels would suddenly come to His aid, whose power and wisdom had knit the very bones of His tormentors together in their mother's wombs, and whose unfathomable mercy was bestowed on them even as they spat upon, mocked, and beat Him, the very Son of God.

In Christ, the will of the Father and the will of the Son were one. His patience was born of the absolute knowledge that He was living and acting in the very center of God's will for Him.

I can of mine own self do nothing : As I hear, I judge: and my judgement is just; because I seek not mine own will, but the will of the Father which hath sent me. (John 5:30)

Christ knew that the will of the Father was being worked in Him and through Him, and He was perfectly obedient, even unto death, to His Father's will.

If we know that we are living and acting in God's will, to whom can we complain when the path seems onerous or burdensome? Rather we should count it all joy knowing this, *"...that the trying of your faith worketh patience." (James 1:3)* It does so because, through our obedience, God reveals more of Himself and His will to us.

How difficult it is at times to see the Father's will through our trials, yet it is impossible to see His will without obedience through our trials. How often have we stopped short and given in to our selfish nature, thereby denying others of that good which God had planned for them through our obedience and denying ourselves the privilege of seeing God's will worked out before our eyes and His faithfulness indelibly impressed on our hearts?

Love is Kind - (OE: cynde - natural)
(Of a friendly, or warmhearted nature. Showing sympathy or understanding)

How unnatural it is for us to be kind, yet that is the original meaning of the word. Perhaps we should think of it as the manner in which we should naturally react to others. We should naturally seek to understand others rather than seeking to be understood by them. We miss so much when we attempt to formulate an answer even before the question is put. To listen with a warm and understanding heart is an art which must be practiced and developed. Jesus spoke of this so subtly yet with words that penetrate to the core of the matter when He said, *"Take heed therefore how ye hear,"* in speaking of the parable of the sower. Here, the seed is God's word, yet the principles of good listening are the same. It is important not so much that we hear but how we hear, and to hear aright, we must first prepare our hearts.

To truly hear with understanding requires an identification with and understanding of another's situation, feelings, and motives. We must vicariously experience their hurt, their joy, their anger, their frustration, their temptation. How easy it is for us to condemn another's sin in an area in which we have not been tempted. We see only their failures and not God's mercy to us in not allowing us to be tempted in a like manner. We boast of our strength when it is God's provision that has kept us strong.

To feel as we feel, it suited our Lord "*...to be made like unto His brethren, that He might be a merciful and faithful high priest...*" (Heb 2:17) Surely He felt the hurt of the leper when He said, "*Lord, if thou wilt, thou canst make me clean.*" (Luke 5:12) The leper knew that Christ could but speak the word, that He could but will that he be healed, and it would be accomplished. He did not ask for a touch, though surely his heart cried out for one. Cast out from society, from those he loved and those who loved him, not even allowed in their presence much less physical contact, he had been without the touch of humankind no doubt for some time.

    Jesus understood the need of his heart as well as his physical need and, with one stroke met them both. Christ heard the lepers words with His ears, but He understood his needs with His heart. The leper asked to be made whole. Most would see the leper's disfigurement and interpret his request as to be cured from his disease, but Jesus knew that the disease had injured much more than his physical body. It had cut him off from the touch, the love, of mankind and wounded his innermost being. His sense of worth, value, and purpose, his deep inner needs, had been denied ever since the priest had uttered that fateful word so long ago; "unclean."

    Little did he know that his knowledge of his worth, value, and purpose would be revealed to him in such a miraculous way. Much less could he have dreamed that it would be revealed at the same time his physical body was made whole. Neither, however, could possibly have taken place without his obedience in turning to Christ as his source of healing, worth, and purpose. In so doing, not only was he made whole physically, emotionally, and spiritually, but he reflected the glorious character of Christ to the world for all generations to read and hear so that others might likewise be healed and reconciled to God. As Jesus saw the leper's physical as well as spiritual and emotional needs, so we must see the needs of others. A good physician knows just the right balm or pill to relieve the pain of our illness, but a great physician removes the very source of the pain. He doesn't stop after asking what hurts. He seeks to understand the cause of the hurt. The great physician goes even further. He feels our hurt as a loving father aches in his very being when the child that he loves hurts. This depth of understanding and feeling only comes with an equal depth of love for others. We must see others as the Savior sees them. We must let our perceptions be filtered through the lens of the mind and the Spirit of Christ.

> *For what man knoweth the things of a man, save the spirit of man which is in him? Even so the things of God knoweth no man, but the spirit of God. Now we have received not the spirit of the world, but the spirit which is of God; that we might know the things that are freely given to us of God. For who hath known the mind of the Lord, that he may instruct him? But we have the mind of Christ.*
> (I Cor 2:11-12,16)

It is the spirit of God within us that allows us to see to the heart of the matter in others' needs. It is the love of God within us that allows us to feel their sadness, their hurt, or their rejection in a personal way. Love is kind because true love truly understands the deep spiritual and emotional needs, as well as the physical needs of others.

David Hume, an eighteenth century philosopher, spoke of the intrinsic connection between the spiritual and the physical nature of man. In his work, "An Enquiry Concerning Human Understanding," he says:

Is there any principle in all nature more mysterious than the union of soul with body; by which a supposed spiritual substance acquires such an influence over a material one, that the most refined thought is able to activate the grossest matter? Were we empowered, by a secret wish, to remove mountains, or control the planets in their orbit, this extensive authority would not be more extraordinary, nor more beyond our comprehension. But if by consciousness we perceive any power, we must know its connection with the effect; we must know the secret union of the soul and body, and the nature of both these substances, by which one is able to operate, in so many instances, upon the other.

How little we understand of the mysteries of the human soul, much less the Spirit of God within us. It is the Spirit which connects us to and makes us individually part of the body of Christ, each part with its necessary function but each part animated by the same Spirit within us. It is the Spirit which allows us to understand the heart of man, "*...for the Lord seeth not as man seeth; for man looketh on the outward appearance, but the Lord looketh on the heart.*" (I Sam 16:7) To treat others with kindness, to truly understand them, we must see with the eyes and hear with the ears of the Spirit.

Love is Not Jealous
(Concerning or arising from feelings of envy, apprehension of loss, or bitterness.)

There is a fascinating depiction of human nature in game theory called *The Prisoner's Dilemma*. The theory attempts to explain and depict human choice as self-utility maximizing; a strategy that bases all conscious decisions on, first and foremost, the meeting of one's desires for self pleasure and gratification. The set up to the game goes like this. Suppose that you were arrested for a crime which you did not commit. After some time, you are brought before the judge. He tells you that there is another individual, whom you have never nor will ever see or know anything further about other than that he is also innocent, that has been incarcerated for the same crime. The judge makes you the following offer. If you accuse the other man of the crime and he, on his part, remains silent, you will be set free and receive a reward and he will remain in jail. If you remain silent and he accuses you, he will be set free and receive the reward and you will remain in jail. If both of you accuse the other, both of you will remain in jail. If both of you remain silent, both of you will be set free.

Game theory attempts to predict and explain the results based purely on the premise that each individual will make a choice that will provide them with the most personal benefit (you go free and receive a reward). This choice, however, leads to the dilemma that, if each prisoner makes this choice, neither one gets what they want and the desires of both are frustrated. The only way the dilemma is potentially resolved is by altering the end game parameters and assuming the game to consist of multiple plays with personal benefits accruing with each successive play. In this manner, the incremental utility of the long term cooperative play would outweigh the one time end game accuse strategy.

What a perfectly rational yet altogether saddening picture of fallen man. The fact that variations of this game were played during Cold War nuclear confrontation scenarios makes this example all the more frightening as a motivational model of human behavior. It is rooted in fear of loss, insecurity, and also envy if we consider as a strategy limiting the utility gained of the opponent, an obvious strategy in the contest for power. We seek comparative advantage over others in terms of wealth, knowledge, or strength in order that we might control the outcome to our advantage and the disadvantage of our enemies. We place our trust in our treasures, our might, and our understanding, and any diminution of these threatens our security. We legitimize and justify our planned or past actions, often regardless of their inherently immoral nature and without a clear understanding of their potential utility in achieving the good which we seek through their use, by claiming that they are necessary to achieve the higher good. In reality, it is more often the individual, personal benefit which we seek.

By doing evil in attempting to achieve good, we

become evil and, what is worse, rationalize that we are not. We discount faith, hope, and love as having any possible usefulness in the 'real' world in which we live and thereby relegate their glory, and that of their author, to the realms of idealist speculation - beautiful in theory but of no practical significance.

In doing so, we foster the very insecurities which we are trying to overcome. If a little wealth makes us somewhat secure, more wealth will make us more secure. If a little prestige gives us pleasure, more prestige is better. In seeking to fill the spiritual void in our lives through temporal means, we find that each successive attainment of our goals leaves us still insecure and wanting. Since these means can never satisfy our deep inner needs, our quest becomes limitless. Is it any wonder that those whose sights are not firmly fixed on Jesus have feelings of jealousy, envy, apprehension, and bitterness?

What a bitter pill it is to find, after struggling a whole lifetime to become successful, sacrificing health, family, friends, and possibly one's very soul, one finds, only too late, that all of this is truly vanity. Love is not jealous because love is rooted in the total confidence that God will supply all of our needs through His riches in glory by Christ Jesus. (Phil 4:19) *"He shall cover thee with His feathers, and under His wings shalt thou trust. His truth shall be thy shield and buckler."* (Ps 91:4) The word picture from this Psalm is of a mother hen with her chicks. The chicks do not know how to meet their own needs. They scurry about, bumping into this and that, and wind up separated from the mother hen. Lost and alone, they cry out, and the mother hen, who was never far away, gently gathers them under her protective wings. If they would only rest there secure, they could avoid the bumps.

Love Does Not Put On Airs
(Is not snobbish)

The word *snob* can be defined in some of the following ways: One who is convinced of and flaunts his social superiority; A person who despises his inferiors and whose condescension arises from social or intellectual pretension; An effort by conformists to express individuality; Pretension - A studied show of superiority.

There are many genres of snobs. There are fashion snobs who will pay exorbitant prices for an item of clothing with a tag bearing a famous designer's name, even if it appears to be no more than a piece of common burlap sewn together. There are intellectual snobs who, of course, prefer to be described as the intellectual elite, this euphemism evidently arising from the fact that only other unknown intellectual elitists have ever heard of them. There are genealogical snobs who frequently refer to their bloodline as if the inheritance of acquired characteristics were still a valid theory. Of course, there are also religious snobs.

Whatever its form, snobbery seeks to make distinctions in comparisons, thereby reinforcing or heightening perceptions of self worth. It boasts of or takes pride in these distinctions, even at times when the distinction is not particularly flattering. It is an effort to express individuality, even if that individuality is, in essence, a type of conformity. Christ was well aware and warned us of man's natural disposition to snobbery. He warned us,

> *Therefore when thou doest thine alms, do not sound a trumpet before thee, as the hypocrites do in the synagogues and in the streets, that they may have glory of men.*
>
> *Verily I say unto you, they have their reward. But when thou doest alms, let not thy right hand know what thy left hand doeth. (Math 6:2-3)*

This is the antithesis of social pretension because it is not men we should be trying to impress nor, for that matter, should we hope to impress God, for He sees to the heart, and the only thing that impresses Him on our behalf is the shed blood of Christ which covers our iniquities. Without this covering, all God sees are the filthy rags of our feeble attempts to earn our own way to righteousness or justification. It is only in humility that we can come before the throne of grace, for *"God resisteth the proud, but giveth grace to the humble," (James 4:6)*

God asks us to do the exact opposite of what our human inclination would have us to do. While we seek a studied show of superiority, God tells us, *"Confess your faults one to another, and pray one for another, that ye may be healed."* (James 5:16) While we seek to accomplish much that we may boast therein, God tells us, *"But he that glorieth, let him glory in the Lord. For not he that commendeth himself is approved, but whom the Lord commendeth."* (II Cor. 10:17-18) We seek comparisons among other men, but God only sees our sin or the righteousness of His son which covers those transgressions. Christ should be our standard of comparison, and being conformed to Him our goal.

All this is not to say that distinctions are useless among men, for God also tells us that we will be known by our fruits. These, however, are self evident and need not be advertised by ourselves. Proverbs 27:2 tells us, *"Let another man praise thee and not thine own lips."* There is an old, tried and true saying: "You can't fool the troops." You may boast of your good deeds and character until the cows come home but, if it is not evidenced in your life, it is, in the final analysis, only self deception. Those who know you best see through the falsehood and, eventually, so will everyone else. Unfortunately, self-deception is pernicious and often more persuasive than the admonishment of friends.

The most difficult part of any healing process is the step requiring the admission that there is a problem. That is why it is so crucial to our acceptance of God's grace to come to the realization that we are all sinners and have all, like sheep, gone astray. Oh that we, like David, could hunger and thirst for righteousness, for when we realize the true state of our natural being, we also realize that it is only through the righteousness of Christ that we can possibly be justified. Then our hearts will be more filled with mercy for those who do not have the restraining influence of the Spirit of God within them. We who are upheld only by the free spirit of Christ, can reconcile others to Him only after we have experienced the joy of our salvation from our sin nature, and this can come only upon the realization that this is our natural state - *"Behold, I was shapen in iniquity; and in sin did my mother conceive me."* (Ps 51:5) Only God, who sees the heart, can create in us a clean heart and renew a right, or constant, spirit within us, for only God is *"...the same yesterday, today, and forever."*

The most disconcerting aspect of snobbishness is that it is so often found in the church. Perhaps this is inevitable as the church, although it is not of the world, is in the world and is therefore affected by its conceptions of honor. Our conceptions of others' worth are often linked to our appraisal of the value of their secular vocations. We are prone to evaluate an individual's ability or worth, even God's ability to use an individual, with an evaluation of their social or economic status or profession. Consciously or unconsciously, we set limits on what individuals, or even groups, are capable of and consequently on what God is able to do through them, by these erroneous conceptions.

God tells us, however, that *"God hath chosen the foolish things of the world to confound the wise; and God hath chosen the weak things of the world to confound the things which are mighty; and base things of the world, and things which are despised, hath God chosen, yea, and things which are not, to bring to naught things that are: that no flesh should glory in His presence."* (I Cor 1:27-29)

How often have we set boundaries on our conceptions of what others could do, thereby quenching the Spirit by setting limits on what He could do through them? How often has the strength of Christ's collective church to effect good been hampered by the schism of doctrines when all agreed on the most important doctrine - Christ and Him crucified and risen? How often have we missed out on God's blessing in seeing His will performed through others by assuming them incapable of any great work? Rather, it is not by power, nor by might, but by the Spirit of God that His will is performed through willing vessels whether those vessels, in and of themselves, have any capability at all, for it is not our ability that God desires but our faithful obedience to be used of Him.

What a relief to realize that we are more than able, through simple, childlike faith, to accomplish whatever God has called us to do. We need not have a high IQ, or great wealth, or high position. We need not strive to become anything except what God has called us to be. Whether we are a corporate CEO or a street sweeper, He has a work for us in that capacity. Our being there is not because of our innate talents, or lack thereof, but because God's providence has put us there to accomplish His divine will, and He can just as easily put us somewhere else. We must learn, like Paul, to be content in whatever situation God, in His infinite wisdom, has decided to put us. It is so easy for us to think in our hearts, *"...my power and the might of my hand hath gotten me this wealth."* (Deut 8:17) We must remember that it is the Lord *" that giveth the power to get wealth, that He may establish His covenant..."* (Deut 8:18)

It is likewise easy for us to think that our failures, lack of ability, or low estate render us useless to God. If we are being faithful to God, we need not worry. We should neither glory in our abilities not cry for their presumed absence, for "

...the race is not to the swift, nor the battle to the strong, neither yet bread to the wise, nor yet riches to men of understanding, nor yet favor to men of skill; but time and chance happeneth to them all." (Eccl 9:11) but, *" the soul that trusts in the Lord shall be established."*

Love is Never Rude
(Ill mannered. Discourteous.
Formed without skill or precision)

Although I believe the first definition to be most consistent with the text, the second is also applicable, for our ill mannered responses to others are often simply emotional reactions which have escaped being filtered through the lens of love or reason. They are delivered without skill or precision if our intent is to address the needs of others. Of course, sometimes they are delivered with excruciating precision to cut to the very heart of others and, in this case, are simply ill mannered or, worse, vindictive.

Collectively, we seem to have lost much by eschewing many of the social graces and courtesies of past ages in the names of free expression, individualism and pragmatic efficiency. We often confuse free expression with plain tactlessness when, out of laziness or simply a lack of concern for the impact our words and actions may have, we fail to frame our expressions in a manner which shows respect for others. This is not a wistful appeal to the past when gentility and social courtesy were the outward expressions of a simpler age, but rather an appraisal of the present in which people seem to have forgotten, or never learned, the social mores which were, in the not too distant past, simply called manners and without which society, much less civil society, would be brutish and quite possibly self-destructive.

Put more simply, good manners are the small, everyday expressions of our commitment to a much larger ethical schema, love, and are the building blocks which form in us the habit of acting in a loving manner. These are the 'lesser ethics,' the practice of which shape our dispositions, habits and character so that, when we are faced with the inevitable ethical crises of life, our practical bent will be toward doing what is right. They are the outward expression of our faithfulness in the smallest expressions of love which equip us to be entrusted with acting faithfully in love's higher callings. Good manners enable good morals. Few have articulated this as succinctly as Edmund Burke:

> *Manners are more important than laws. Upon them, in great measure, the laws depend. The law touches us but here and there, now and then. Manners are what vex or sooth, corrupt or purify, exalt or debase, barbarize or refine us, by a constant, steady, uniform, insensible operation like that of the air we breathe. They give their whole form and color to our lives. According to their quality, they aid morals, they supply them, or they totally destroy them.*
> (Letters on a Regicide Peace, I, 1796)

The written, positive law serves to codify the moral ethic, thereby providing specific substance to the general conception of right and wrong, backing it with legitimate, temporal authority. As the written law evolves from the unwritten moral standard, so this standard derives its solidity and efficacy from those habits of social interaction which may collectively be called our manners. Changes in both our laws and our manners, therefore, are the visible expressions of changes in the ethical standards which provide them.

Many of the changes in our contemporary laws and manners have arisen due to misconceptions and perversions of the doctrines of liberty and justification. The liberty of individual conscience guided by the word through the agency of the Holy Spirit has become perverted, by its secularization, to a radical individualism that knows not the bounds of selfless love but only the boundlessness of desire, will, and appetite. We must remember Paul's words of warning to the Galatians,

> *Ye have been called to liberty: only use not liberty for an occasion to the flesh, but by love serve one another. For all the law is fulfilled in one word, even this; thou shalt love thy neighbor as thyself.* (Gal 5:13-14)

Likewise, he warns the Corinthians,

> *All things are lawful for me, but all things are not expedient. All things are lawful for me, but all things edify not. Let no man seek his own, but every man another's wealth.* (I Cor 10:23-24)

To the Romans he writes,

> *It is good neither to eat flesh, not to drink*

> *wine, nor anything whereby thy brother stumbleth, or is offended, or is made weak.* (Rom 14:21)

Likewise, although we are not justified by works, but by faith, our faith is made complete by our works of love. (Gal 5:6) It is through this working out of our faith by our daily acts of love to others that God shows Himself to be ever present, active, and faithful. It is by being obedient in the small things that we are enabled to be obedient in the larger things. It is only by first learning to follow that we may learn to lead. It is only by learning to listen that we may learn to answer aright. It is only by learning the basics of love - sympathy, kindness, consideration, and the host of other petty sacrifices that make up good manners - that we can, with skill and precision, use these building blocks to construct lasting, loving relationships.

Love is Not Self-Seeking

The gift of love and the gift of the capacity to love are two of the greatest mysteries as well as most beneficent acts of our heavenly Father to humankind. It is beyond the capacity of our human minds to conceive of how a perfect God could choose to sacrifice His only son, a sacrifice made equally for all, for imperfect, sinful creatures such as we. It is equally difficult to comprehend the paradox of the kind of love that we are called to exhibit - love that is equally completely selfless yet manifested within a nature so driven by personal needs and their fulfillment. An understanding of the gift and the apparent paradox will elude us unless we understand the nature of man, beginning with the premise that he is not only a physical and mental being, but a spiritual being as well. When we recognize that man is, in his nature, composed of mind, body, and also spirit, the difficulty becomes resolvable.

Just as love has many characteristics but selflessness is the most descriptive, so man has several innate characteristics but his spiritual nature and needs are the most descriptive of him as, first, they are the only permanent part of his makeup and, second, they govern, to a large extent, the expressions of his other potentialities. It is the limitless nature of the spirit of man and his quest for the fulfillment of its potentialities which, apart from being fulfilled in God, drive him to the boundless pursuit of mere pleasure, hoping thereby to be satisfied. Because the spiritual needs of man are of such great influence, gross errors are brought about when they are disregarded, not only in our understanding of ourselves and others, but also in fundamental issues concerning prescriptive truths and our ability to fulfill the dictates of these truths.

Prescriptive truths are those which, because they state how things ought to be and not how they actually exist in objective reality, must be self-evident to claim the mantle of truth. This self-evidence consists in the impossibility of conceiving the opposite of what is stated. For instance, the truth that we ought to desire what is really good for us and nothing else unless these additional 'goods' do not interfere with our obtaining what is really good for us is self-evident. It is impossible to conceive of the truth of the opposite proposition - that we ought to desire what is really bad for us. This self-evident truth puts us under the moral obligation, assuming we are free moral agents, to seek what is really good for us.

What is really good for us is that which we, by nature, need as equally created human beings, equal in the sense that we all possess in equal measure those potentialities which distinguish us from other creatures At this point, self-evidence leaves us and we must look to objectively evidenced human nature to determine, specifically, what those real goods are which we ought all to desire.

This is also the point at which the grievous error is made of discounting the spiritual nature of man due to the seeming impossibility of objectively experiencing its expression. It is quite easy to accept, that man, because of his physical being, needs those things which sustain life. These are real goods for him. It is also easy to accept that man, because of his mental nature and capacity to learn, needs knowledge. This is a real good for him. It is much more difficult to accept, because of his spiritual nature, man's innate potentiality to acquire spiritual wisdom - the knowledge of the reality of God obtained through experiencing Him in our daily lives. If spiritual wisdom is, in fact, a real good (something that we need by nature because it is an innate potentiality), then we are under a moral obligation which is categorical to seek it. Whether we accept this as truth or not makes it no less true.

Herein lies the great mystery of love. **The knowledge of the reality of God can only be objectively evidenced to us through our exercise of faith in and obedience to God.** As we are obedient in showing His love to others, God manifests Himself to us and, in so doing, fulfills our innate spiritual need to know Him and experience Him in our daily lives.

By considering other's needs as more important than our own, and by forsaking our own apparent needs in consideration of others, we show them God's love and help them to experience His reality. It is only when we are obedient to God in selflessly sharing His love with others that He reveals Himself to us, thereby fulfilling our deep, spiritual need to know Him. **The objective reality of our innate, spiritual need to know God can-**

not be objectively demonstrated without faith and obedience.

As the commandment to love is an all encompassing commandment, without being obedient in love through faith we cannot know God. Without love, we are truly nothing, for without being obedient in love we cannot know God.

One might argue that love is not selfless if it is motivated by a desire to fulfill one's personal needs, even though the nature of the acts may appear selfless. To be obedient in love, however, requires that we truly are selfless. We must truly desire the good of others above our own. As God sees the heart, He also knows if we are truly being obedient in love, and this is another great mystery, for it is humanly impossible - beyond our nature - to be able to love as we ought.

It is only by allowing the Spirit of God within us to love through us that we can truly love as we ought. The gift of the capacity to love as we ought is the gift of the Spirit of God within us. It is the Spirit which shapes the desires of our heart so that we desire aright, and it is only by loving through the empowerment of the Holy Spirit within us that we can truly be obedient in love, experience the reality of God in our daily lives, and attain the spiritual wisdom which we all need by nature. The paradox is that we can only verify this innate potentiality by first being obedient, for it is only through obedience that God reveals Himself to us.

This is not to say that there is not sufficient evidence of the existence of God without our obedience, for...

the invisible things of him from the creation of the world are clearly seen, being understood by the things that are made, even his eternal power and godhead; ... (Rom 1:20)

This, however, is much different from the knowledge of an ever present, loving Father who is constantly involved and at work in the daily activities of our lives, shaping our desires so that we might selflessly love as we ought and truly know Him

Love is Not Easily Provoked
Does Not Take Offense

A person's feelings are such a delicate, changeable, and unpredictable thing. One moment we may feel on top of the world and the next, because of a caustic statement by a boss, a lover, or a friend, that feeling of elation is transformed, in a moment, from apprehension, to sadness, to anger. How could they say such things? Don't they know how hard I'm trying? Am I really good for nothing? How dare they! Who do they think they are anyway?

Of course, quite often these questions simply simmer within us and are not given verbal expression. The outward expression of these feelings may be limited to a less than stellar performance on the task at hand, avoidance of the offending party, small talk to co-workers about the boss's total lack of understanding of the problem, or the physical venting of anger on or with inanimate objects. Often, it is only when we get home to those whom we really love and trust that we give full vent to our feelings of loss of worth or value and anger. After all, if you can't take it out on your family, on whom can you take it out? You've got plenty to be mad at them for. The children never close a door or drawer. Whatever they use winds up right on the floor, just where they stopped using it. They don't respect the value of anything. They can be so destructive. That new car we got - I still can't believe how much we paid for it - has already gotten bubble gum stuck in the carpet, and the dent from the baseball - Oh! I could just.... Pretty soon, we forget what it was that made us feel angry in the first place, and all those pent up feelings are bearing down on Happy Valley Circle on their unwitting victims. As you pull into the driveway, Johnny bounces a long jump shot off the rim and - WHAM! - it lands on the hood right next to the not so old baseball dent. All of a sudden, all the negative feelings of the day, the week, are focused on one target of opportunity as he walks right into your crosshairs with a sheepish grin - Gee, sorry Dad. Bad shot. Looks like it didn't make another dent though! The picture doesn't need to be completed. We've all been there, either as the worker, the little boy or girl, or as the parent, and we've all learned, some better than others and either from the giving or receiving end, ways to cope with anger, either theirs or ours. Part of this coping process is learning not only how to deal with the feeling, but the root causes that generate the feeling.

Anger is a natural emotion. We all experience it. It is a natural reaction when we view or experience those things which go contrary to the way we think they ought to go, the way we expect them to go, or the way we desire them to go. The problem with anger is not that we have the feeling, but why we have the feeling and how we respond to that feeling. That anger is a natural, God-given emotion is attested to by the instances of God's righteous anger recorded in His word. The Word tells us that, "God is angry with the wicked every day." (Ps 7:11 There are also many particular instances of

God's anger. He often became angry with His chosen people, Israel, because they had turned away from Him and disregarded His commandments. He became angry with the money changers in the temple saying, "Is it not written, 'My house shall be called a house of prayer for all nations?', but you have made it a den of thieves." He became angry with Solomon because, even after having appeared to him on two occasions, his heart had turned away from his God. (I Kings 11:9) The many instances of God's anger throughout the scripture, as well as the scriptural admonishment against man's anger, require us to search out, in regards to our own behavior, what constitutes the core difference between righteous and sinful anger.

As anger arises from frustrated expectations or desires, the difference must lie in the realm of our expectations and desires, the frustration of which give rise to the feelings or emotions of anger, righteous or unrighteous. If the anger arises from the frustration of unrighteous expectations or desires, it cannot be without sin. If our expectations, hopes, and desires are rooted in love, the more common emotion associated with their frustration will be sadness as we experience others acting contrary to that manner which would bring about what is really good for them and others. The words of Christ as He hung on the cross are illustrative of this point: *"Father, forgive them for they know not what they do."*

God's righteous anger is kindled against us when we knowingly and willfully act contrary to what He has clearly revealed to us to be the manner in which we should act. For man's anger to be righteous then, it must proceed first from a heart of love and, second, from a knowledge of the heart of others. If we truly desire the best for others, when this desire is frustrated by others unknowingly acting in a manner which is inappropriate to the attainment of their personal happiness or the happiness of others, we will experience sadness, not anger. What is more, the degree of our sadness will be commensurate with the strength of our desire and love, as our emotional reactions are always most passionate in regards to those things about which we care deeply. Additionally, this sadness is not something which we choose to feel, but is rather the natural and necessary reaction to the frustration of our desires. This is why it has been said that feelings are neither right nor wrong, and neither good nor bad. They just are. There are, however, righteous and unrighteous desires, and it is in their fulfillment or frustration that these emotions arise.

The requirement that we know the heart, the motivations and inner intent, of others in their actions of anger renders most human emotions of anger unrighteous unless, of course, the motivations and inner intent are clearly manifested to us either by the actor or the Spirit. The double requirement that righteous anger be motivated by love makes it even more rare. The further admonishments that we be angry and sin not and also be slow to anger (Ephes 4:26) render the great majority of our expressions of anger if not clearly sinful at least less than righteous if there be a difference.

The enormous destructive potential of the

human emotion of anger, both to the individual who harbors this emotion as well as to whom it is directed, is only consistent with a very narrow definition of anger which can be considered righteous. That the cultivation of this emotion eventually leads to its development into hate, the opposite of love, should motivate us to avoid it at all costs. Just as love covers a multitude of sins, so anger can generate in us a multitude of sins, especially when we deceive ourselves into the belief that our anger is justified by what we perceive to be the malevolent intent of others. The motivations and inner intent of others is only one determinant of the righteous or unrighteous character of our anger.

Our own motivation, whether it is based on love or concern for the needs of others, is also determinant. It is for these very reasons that we are admonished, time and again, to be slow to anger that we might avoid not only the sin of unrighteous anger but the cascade of resulting errors that inevitably follow.

None of the foregoing is meant to suggest that we should never have the emotion of anger or that we are incapable of righteous anger. Again, if it were inappropriate, it would not have been evidenced in our Lord. The dual prerequisite of love and insight into the motivations of others is not something unattainable. A mother's natural love for her children and her anger at those who maliciously design and carry out actions that are clearly hurtful to them is not only righteous but very closely resembles the anger of our loving Father in heaven towards those who would intentionally, and with a clear understanding of their error, lead His elect astray.

    The anger of Christ towards the Pharisees, those to whom the word of God had been clearly revealed and yet who still clung to their worldly desires, was plain. What is also plain is that Christ's anger was always tempered with mercy, love, and forgiveness, and this is the point at which we frequently fail, for we often forget that, even though others may deserve our righteous anger, we are still commanded to love them and, from this love, show them mercy and forgiveness. This too is what is meant by the Word where we are admonished to be angry and sin not, for even if our anger is righteous, if we do not also have room in our heart for mercy, love, and forgiveness we are not without sin. It is righteous anger, tempered by mercy and forgiveness because it originates in love, that shapes our reactions to this powerful emotion and allows us to channel it into constructive responses. It is the perception of the Spirit within us, as well, that allows us to see to the heart of others so that our responses will be most effective in eliciting the changes in and for others which will bring about what is really good for them and which are motivated by our truly desiring what is best for them. Is it any wonder that we are cautioned to be slow to anger? It takes time to understand others' feelings. It takes time to listen to the Spirit's urgings. It takes time to search out the Father's guidance through His word. It takes time and patience to await the answer and the proper moment that God has set to respond. It takes time for God to prepare the hearts of others to listen. It takes time to give mercy and forgiveness a chance to elicit God's desired response in the hearts of others and for these inner decisions to find their expression in changed behavior. It takes time for God to prepare us to be the instruments of change in the circumstances or environment which elicited our righteous anger and, if our anger be righteous and our love strong, we will not shrink from the effort. These are the fruits of righteous anger; acts of mercy and forgiveness, changed hearts, repentance, and dedicated, untiring, persistent effort to understand and to change those things which God had shown us to require to be changed.

If He has clearly revealed to us those things which should be changed, and He has indeed if we have truly experienced righteous anger, then what should we expect if we act contrary to what He has clearly revealed to us? Be angry and sin not. Be angry and love. Be angry and forgive. Be angry and show mercy. Be angry and allow God to help you channel that emotion into those works which He has before ordained that you should walk in as instruments of change.

Love Does Not Rejoice at Wrong

It might seem an easy thing to avoid rejoicing over sin. It is, after all, contrary to the very term *Christian* to consider that one called by that name could rejoice in what is wrong. That assumes a perfection in love, however, which is unfortunately lacking in each of us in varying degrees and at various times. If we consider the characteristic of love as described in I Corinthians 8:1 that "...love builds up," we can easily see how this is so by understanding how love builds up. To build up in a spiritual sense, love, being the deepest ground of the life of the spirit, must be the foundation. How can we build up each other in love? We can do so either by implanting that love in the hearts of others or by so ordering our thoughts, emotions, and actions towards them that we presuppose this foundation to be already in place and, in love, respond by building upon it accordingly. As only God, who is love, has the power to inspire us with His Spirit of love, it is humanly impossible for us to implant love in the heart of another. But we can build upon the foundation which He has laid and of which He is the cornerstone. This presupposition of love, then, and the natural consequences which this assumption brings, are all that are left to us if we are to build up one another in love.

How often we misperceive the intentions of others and, because of that misperception and the assumption of hurtful intent on the part of others towards us, tear each other down. Love, on the contrary, assumes the best intentions in others, regardless of appearances, and responds in love. So many hurtful episodes, many of which escalate and assume a character totally out of proportion to the original incident, could be avoided by this simple assumption and understanding is inevitably gained as real communication is allowed to continue.

Much sin could also be avoided by holding the opinion that others bear us no hurtful intent, for by assuming otherwise, we adopt a self-righteous attitude towards them and feel justified in pointing out their faults, deceiving ourselves that we are thus building them up in love by pointing out their sin. We rejoice in the false belief that "we are not like these other sinners," and in the equally false belief that, by pointing out their faults, we have done our duty. The exact opposite is the reality. We have erred, and erred greatly, because we have failed to build up in love.

Of course, it is possible to know the heart of others either when this has been revealed to us by the actors themselves or by the Spirit. The knowledge of hurtful intent on the part of others, however, does not absolve us from the command to love and, as with righteous anger, our actions should still seek to build up, even though the hurt be great, and in that response, hope and pray that God will water the seed sown to lay a foundation of love in their heart.

This does not mean that others should be absolved from the just consequences of their actions, but that the intent of these consequences should always be based upon achieving their real and eternal good, and the temporary or temporal sorrow which these consequences bring should never elicit anything but compassion, a constant hope for repentance, and an equal willingness to show mercy and forgive. When we rejoice because others have received a just recompense for their misconduct, not because justice has been upheld or their regeneration possibly begun but because we derive some misguided sense of pleasure or satisfaction in the fact that they have suffered equally to the suffering they have caused, we rejoice in sin. To say that this is only human is no excuse. Love, on the contrary, rejoices with the truth. Love rejoices when the revelation and acknowledgement of truth to and by those who have transgressed it and caused others harm elicits repentance and changed behavior, whether they suffer punishment equal to the harm they have caused or not. Love welcomes the repentant back with open arms and heart and rejoices, forgetting the transgression in the joy of finding that which was lost. Thank God that we are well represented in God's court of justice, for if we all received what justice demands, we would all be lost.

Love Bears All Things

Galatians 6:2 tells us to "Bear ye one another's burdens and so fulfill the law of Christ." These burdens may be physical, mental, or spiritual. Love bears them all. So often it is the physical burdens alone that we see and these, to be sure, are important. If we see a brother in need, we are not to look away from that need. We are to feed those who are hungry, shelter those who are homeless, cloth those who are naked, and heal those who are sick. To show concern for another's spiritual welfare without also showing concern for their physical as well as mental welfare is a mockery of love. Love seeks what is really good for another's mental and physical as well as spiritual well being.

This, in fact, is the wisdom of love. Long before the term "holistic medicine" was coined, love showed the way to real healing. For healing to be real, it must include one's whole being, for just as the miracle of forgiveness cannot be realized until one allows oneself to be forgiven, even so physical healing is seldom complete and lasting until ones mental and spiritual dimensions are also made whole. It is a well known fact that we can make ourselves physically sick from a 'broken heart,' or a broken spirit. Conversely, the old saying that laughter is good medicine is also well founded. Long before modern medicine, Solomon declared *"A merry heart doeth good like medicine; but a broken spirit drieth the bones."* (Prov 17:22)

Perhaps the reason we focus more on the physical dimension is because of its tangible nature. It is easy to see the results when we provide for another's physical needs. It is also, at times, much easier for us to provide for those needs and then to relax with a sense of having done one's duty. But love calls for us to go beyond mere duty and to embrace selfless service.

Whom would a child call father? One who provided for his every physical need but with whom there existed no relationship except for financial support, or one who raised him, who was there to talk with, to share hopes and dreams with as well as disappointments and joys? Love calls for more than the mere provision of needs. It calls for the establishment of relationships, and these take time, energy, and real effort.

It is unlikely that we shall ever know what the burdens of others are unless such a relationship is formed. What is also more than probable is that our own development in love will never be complete unless we are willing to open our hearts to others, forming these relationships. This is the very point which holds us back from making that commitment to love and, in love, bear all.

Loving relationships assume certain obligations and constraints. They constrain our liberty. It is not only our conscience that we must worry about, but we must also seek not to offend another's conscience. It is not our needs which hold priority, but others needs. Our own hopes and dreams are no longer important except as they are shared hopes and dreams or sought in relation to attaining the real good of the other. Our liberty to 'do as we please so long as it doesn't hurt anyone' is transformed to our freedom from the chains of selfish desire with its endless quest for satisfaction to serving others because this is now our pleasure.

Kris Kristopherson got it half right when he said, "*Freedom's just another word for nothing' left to loose.*"

The phrase, incomplete as it is, has a sorrowful tone. It must be completed to reveal its full meaning - love has nothing left to loose because it has given everything that it has and, in that giving, found all that it really ever needed.

Love Believes All Things
(There is no limit to love's trust)
Hopes All Things
Endures All Things

These are very difficult characteristics of love to exemplify. They seem to say that, although we may bear all things, fully believing that our love will receive no recompense from the one loved, loving in fact in spite of this belief, if we love in this manner, our love is without trust, without hope, and incomplete.

This, however, cannot be so, for Christ's love was perfect and offered equally for all even while He knew that all would not accept this love. The object of our limitless trust and hope in love can only be God, for *He alone can be trusted to be always able, always true, and always sure to reward our obedience in love by more fully revealing Himself to us.*

There is no limit to love's trust and hope because there is nothing that can limit God's faithfulness to us when we put our trust in Him. In fact, God Himself is constrained by His very character and His word. God is always true to His word. If He were not, He would be acting contrary to His very nature, and His word clearly tells us that, if we trust in Him, He *will* direct our paths.

Understanding and accepting this does not, however, make it easy, for God's timing is not our timing, nor are His ways our ways, and at times we must trust even when all of our senses tell us that our efforts are for naught. But if we wait on the Lord, He shall renew our strength by allowing us to clearly see Him reveal Himself to us. We must look forward to that revelation with confidence and expectation, hoping even when all hope seems lost and our hope appears to others as mere foolishness and we but dreamers. We must let our hearts hear the "sound of the abundance of rain" though all around us tell us that "there is nothing," and we must prepare for God's response, for, in the meanwhile, as we act on that faith, God will bring a rain of blessing. (I Kings 18:41-46)

Love Never Fails

Love always secures that which it seeks. The truth of this statement is difficult to understand unless love is understood as obedience, for there are many instances and example of unrequited love. Even the love of Christ which seeks to draw all men to Himself does not succeed in doing so as many will not accept this love.

Love, however, never fails because God never fails when we act in obedience to Him by expressing His love to others through the empowerment of the Spirit within us. God is always faithful and true to His word, and His word tells us that love never fails. The succeeding verses explain what the success of love consists of. They don't speak of love being returned to the one who shows love, nor do they speak of this love miraculously changing the hearts of others, although both of these things could happen. No, what they speak of is the continued, personal revelation of God to the one who loves in obedience to Him. This is why God's word says that love never fails.

God is always faithful in revealing more of Himself to us when we act in obedience to Him. As God's nature is infinite, it is impossible that this revelation can ever be complete in this life. His faithfulness is great and His mercies are new every morning. The revelation is a continuous process. Love never fails because there is always more of God to be revealed to us until we are perfected in love in His presence. Then we will know God in all His fullness and glory and have unbroken communion with Him.

How little we understand of the infinite glory, power and majesty of God. Now we see in part, and that part is expanded only through our continued faith in and obedience to God. Our growth in spiritual wisdom - the knowledge of the reality of God as a personal, loving Father who is active in and through our lives - is a lifelong process that will continue until we are perfected in Him.

www.ingramcontent.com/pod-product-compliance
Lightning Source LLC
Chambersburg PA
CBHW021122080526
44587CB00010B/603